LEADERSHIP
THAT MAKES AN
IMPACT

Carl W. Basden

ISBN 979-8-88851-367-5 (Paperback)
ISBN 979-8-88851-368-2 (Digital)

Covenant Books
11661 Hwy 707
Murrells Inlet, SC 29576
www.covenantbooks.com

CONTENTS

ACKNOWLEDGMENTS

Special thanks to my wonderful wife, Sharia, who has made an incredible impact on me, our family, and so many others. She has willingly made many sacrifices and adjustments throughout my career and our marriage. She has been my chief supporter and encourager.

Thanks to all three of my children—DeAnna Hammond, Allyson Brimer, and Will Basden—for allowing me to use some of their childhood stories for illustrations in this book. I am immensely proud of them and the leaders they have become. They have certainly made a positive impact on my life!

INTRODUCTION

Several years ago, I attended an executive education program at Louisiana State University. The instructor in one of the classes asked us to introduce ourselves and, in a word or two, explain our leadership philosophy. I knew integrity was important to me, and that was what I shared. Some of the students had obviously thought through this more than I had, and some even had some acronyms they used to describe their philosophies. I was impressed! I asked myself why I was not able to articulate my thoughts as clearly. I began to work on developing a leadership philosophy, one that I could explain to anyone when called upon. I started making a list of the values that were important to me. I wanted them to be practical and easily understood. In addition, I wanted them to be easy to remember. The purpose of this book is to share the outcome of that effort. I hope that the resulting leadership model will prove to be beneficial for you as you lead your organization.

The components of the model are as follows:

- *I*ntegrity
- *M*otivation
- *P*erformance
- *A*ttitude
- *C*ommunication
- *T*eamwork

In the following chapters, we will dig into the different words in an attempt to explain why each component is an essential factor in a leader's effectiveness. As you read the explanations about why each component is important, I challenge you to begin to open your mind to how you can utilize these simple principles to help you make an impact on others and enhance your effectiveness as a leader.

CHAPTER 1

Integrity

Integrity is foundational! It cannot be compromised!

In the early 2000s, I had the opportunity to receive executive coaching from the Turknett Leadership Group in Atlanta, Georgia. This firm provides leadership training to executives from many companies in the Atlanta area and beyond. They use a model that communicates the importance of balancing respect and responsibility. The foundation for the model, though, is integrity. The Turknett Leadership Group says, "Character is grounded in integrity. Without it, no leader can be successful. Leaders must be honest, authentic, and completely trustworthy. A person with integrity doesn't twist facts for personal advantage. He or she stands for what is right, keeps all promises and always tells the truth. A person with integrity is able to make sound decisions, even when faced with temptation or conflict."[1]

Our character is the basis for everything that we do. John Morley said, "No man can climb out beyond the limitations of his own character."[2] In other words, we cannot pretend to be something that we are not. People are smart! They can see through false pretense.

Tell the Truth

Leaders must tell the truth. Leaders should avoid falling into the trap of just telling people what they want to hear. We have all seen leaders who twist the facts or just simply avoid telling the truth out of fear that the truth will tarnish his/her image. In his book, *Patton on Leadership*, Alan Axelrod said, "The truth will prevail, one way or another, and usually sooner rather than later. It is better to face it now and to convince others to do the same."[3]

Not only should leaders always tell the truth, but they should also expect the same from the people in their organization. In an effective organization, there should be an absolute freedom to tell the truth. Almost all employees would prefer to tell the truth, but they must be empowered to do so. The employee must know that the truth can be accepted no matter how bad the news may be. Failure to give employees this power will destroy trust in the leadership.

Avoid Compromising Your Values

Why did the Turknett Leadership Group feel compelled to mention the importance of decision-making during times of temptation? The leader faces plenty of temptation in the daily rigors of running the business. Let's look at an example that reaches across most industries.

In today's business world, there are always pressures to reduce costs. One of the biggest cost components for companies is people. When companies look for ways to reduce costs, they invariably start looking at how to reduce the number of employees. Utilizing contract firms to perform some functions becomes an alternative that has to be considered. While contract companies can offer many benefits, they also can present a number of challenges, many times testing the integrity of leaders. As firms jockey for consideration, they may offer favors or kickbacks to the decision makers.

Most companies today provide ethics training to assist their employees in understanding the rights and wrongs in business relationships. But leaders should have a predetermined conviction to do the right thing and be able to recognize when they are being asked to compromise on that position.

Here are a few guidelines that I always gave a new organization about dealing with contractors:

- Integrity should always be at the core of what we do.
- Business controls must be in place when you engage a contractor. Be clear about the task to be performed and what will be paid for the work requested. Documentation of the key components is always required.
- Always have an approved contract with an approved vendor.

- Always be sure the contract price is consistent with the work performed and in accordance with the contract.
- Avoid doing business with vendors based on family ties, friendships, or former coworker relationships.

When representatives of contract companies met with me to ask for my business, they had to sit through the same speech every time: "I have a pretty simple set of expectations. I expect to receive a quality product performed on time for a fair price. If you are able to do those three things consistently, there will likely be some opportunity. But the most important attribute that must be exhibited is integrity. If you do not display integrity, you cannot work here, plain and simple!"

I made it clear that I did not tell my team who they should use or who they should not use to get the work performed unless I had personal knowledge that the company had integrity issues. If I knew they did, then I would ban them from performing work for our organization. Integrity is too important! You cannot allow it to be compromised!

Practice Ethical Conduct

Almost all companies have human resource departments that spend a lot of time training employees on how to conduct themselves in challenging situations and maintain proper business ethics. Invariably, employees have lapses that are just inexplicable. Those lapses may be where they just used poor judgment and either did or said something in poor taste.

I had numerous situations where an employee said something that was inappropriate, including instances of racial, sexual, or threatening content. Many times, the employee would explain it by saying, "Oh, it was just a joke. Everyone in the room knew that I was not serious." And in fact, it may be true that everyone in the room did laugh. But a few months later, when someone lost their job and filed suit, it was no longer found to be funny. I sat in a number of depositions and saw attorneys take quotes from a naive employee and just bear down on the company representative trying to defend the conduct.

Much of the time, the conduct was impossible to defend. I always gave counsel to my team that went like this: "Things that might seem funny when the employee is among peers are not nearly as funny when you are sitting in a deposition."

Leaders have to instill within their employees that the rules of business ethics in the human resources policies and procedures are there for a reason. Employees must take the policies seriously and adhere to them.

Ensure Consistency

Leading with integrity means that there has to be a consistent message from leadership regardless of the audience. Leaders have to support the people on their team. They should never undermine the people they are counting on to execute the plan.

Let me give you an illustration of what I am talking about. When I was a fairly new manager, our leadership was placing a lot of emphasis on the need to improve technician productivity. The midlevel managers had to meet with senior leadership once a quarter to explain the results and defend why the performance was not up to par. We had to give an account of the number of entries for poor performance that we had put into employees' records and were challenged on why there were not more technicians on a disciplinary plan for poor performance.

In these meetings, there were even threats that some managers were going to lose their jobs if they were not diligently administering the plan. I was a young manager and was doing my best to implement the plan as it had been communicated. I was insisting that the supervisors who reported to me follow the plan to the letter. Needless to say, it was not a popular subject with the employee body.

The vice president responsible for the territory decided to visit one of my work locations. It just happened that the location selected was where some of the poorest performers were located. These employees were definitely feeling the pressures of the performance improvement plan.

After the vice president's brief talk about the state of the business, he opened up the floor for questions. The technicians immediately began to express their frustrations over the pressure to improve their performance. One technician complained about how stressful the job had become and how, for the first time in his career, he was afraid that he might lose his job.

The response from the vice president was astonishing to me. Understand that he had been in these quarterly meetings with the managers and had participated in grilling the managers about why they were not putting more entries in people's records for poor performance. He said, "We need all of you. We've invested a lot in you. I don't know why you should be concerned about your job."

He failed to point out how important it was for every business to become more efficient and for every employee to become more productive. He failed to point out that making those improvements would keep the company competitive and allow them to keep good-paying jobs so they could provide for their families. By the time he finished, it was pretty clear that I was the bad guy. It seemed that I was pushing my own agenda of improving productivity. What do you think that did for my standing in the group? What did it tell me about his integrity?

I learned a valuable lesson that day and I told myself that I would never be guilty of being so weak and unsupportive of my frontline managers. To my knowledge, I never failed to support openly what I was expecting the management team to accomplish. The failure of an executive to stand up and face the truth is a failure of leadership. You cannot expect lower- and middle-level managers to administer a plan that you are unwilling to defend when in front of the frontline employees. Just explain to them why the improvements you are seeking are important. Improving productivity is a key component for a company to succeed, especially in a competitive environment. People are smart!

They can understand and respect the truth. But they can spot weakness a mile away, and they will use it against you.

The employees in an organization observe the conduct of the leader. They clearly pick up on what is important, and it establishes the basis for an organization's culture. If employees at any level learn that the leader does not have integrity, that leader is viewed as ineffective. It is next to impossible to overcome a lapse in integrity. Remember, it cannot be compromised. There is a reason it is the first word in the model!

CHAPTER 2

Motivation

Most leaders understand the importance of being able to motivate their employees. But many struggle with how to do it. As a leader, it is important that you are motivated. How do you approach the job? When employees see that the leader is motivated, they are much more likely to follow.

Embrace Opportunity

Many organizations can rock along pretty well when things are on a routine course.

The true test of a leader's ability to motivate his/her employees is when times are challenging. Difficulties are sure to come, and every leader will be put to the test.

Do you see opportunities in every difficulty or difficulties in every opportunity?

I like to tell the story about my daughters and a conversation they had when they were young children. I was outside, mowing my backyard. It was cloudy, and an afternoon thunderstorm began brewing. I was going to be out of town the next week and was determined to get the yard mowed before the rain came. The sky darkened, and we began to experience a lot of lightning. DeAnna, who was five at the time, was a worrier. She began to cry and told her mother, "Daddy needs to quit mowing. He is going to get struck by lightning! He is going to die! You will have to get married again!" Allyson, who was three at the time, had been listening to her sister; and she also got excited. She raised her hand and said, "I can be the flower girl!" See, she had this desire to be the flower girl in a wedding, and she was ready to seize the opportunity.

While that is just a humorous family story that we have always remembered, it does depict a person's outlook when they run into difficulties. It is not always going to be smooth sailing. How a leader responds to challenges greatly affects how the team will be motivated to work through those challenges.

Provide Focus and Direction

It is the leader's job to provide focus and direction. Your people have to know where you are going. There is a Japanese proverb that says, "Vision without action is a daydream. Action without vision is a nightmare." The most effective way to instill the vision is to have an annual strategy alignment process. The leaders at the highest level determine the key components of a plan that will lead to success in the current year and beyond. That strategy should then be cascaded down through the organization, with each division determining how what they do every day can impact the plan and lead to their supervisor's success. The goal is for the frontline employees to understand how the work they perform every day is important to the overall success of the firm. If employees understand how much their job matters, they are much more likely to take pride in their performance and be motivated to improve.

Lead with Empathy

One of the biggest challenges that I faced when trying to motivate an organization was when that organization had to navigate through force reductions. We went through periods where business was strong and it seemed that we could not hire people fast enough. Invariably, we would then hit the difficult times of economic downturns when we had to reduce the workforce. Both of those instances presented difficulties for the leadership, but reducing forces was by far the most difficult for me.

Early in my tenure as a manager, we went through an organizational change where we moved essentially all the functions performed by the group that I managed to a central location in the state. Almost everyone in the organization was affected in some way. Many of the employees had always lived at that location and had as many as twenty-five years or more with the company. Most of them had the opportunity to follow their work to the new location, but it meant that they would have to relocate. For some employees, relocation was not a viable option for multiple reasons. It might be because of their spouse's job, after-school childcare, or their unwillingness to leave their home.

I worked countless hours, listening to employee concerns and trying to find them other job opportunities to stay with the company. I had empathy for their situations, different as they all were. In addition, I was busy making plans for the new location, where I also would be moving.

In the midst of this turmoil, I was discussing some of the employee issues with my boss. He said, "You are allowing yourself to become too emotionally involved with this surplus situation." I was a bit stunned. I remember what I told him. I said, "I hope that I never have a group of employees go through a force reduction where I am not bothered by the upheaval that it causes them and their families."

I went through numerous initiatives like this over my career. I never went through one of them, without thinking about that conversation. Leaders do not have to come across as calloused and unsympathetic to conditions that are concerning to employees. In fact, quite the opposite is true. Employees need to see the human side of the leader and see that he/she cares. That makes leaders stronger, not weaker!

Have Fun

It is hard to motivate employees if the work cannot be fun. It is important to be able to have fun at work. Some leaders do not believe they can be focused on the job and still have fun. Those leaders have no clue how to motivate people. I believe in hard work. But I believe you can work hard and still have fun. We need to be willing to laugh with others and at ourselves.

Following Hurricane Katrina in 2005, I was responsible for leading the organization in restoring telephone service for BellSouth customers on the Mississippi Gulf Coast. I have never faced a bigger challenge. The devastation was incredible. The destruction to the local businesses and residences in the area was overwhelming. My heart was broken for the many employees and their families whose homes were damaged or destroyed. I had great admiration and respect for how those employees worked long hours on the job and then went home, attempted to patch things together, and lead their families.

Even in the midst of the huge challenges confronting the workforce, we had numerous things happen that were just really funny. We were able to laugh, and it was good for us all. It's amazing how good it feels and how much tension is released when you have a good laugh.

One of our engineering directors was a hands-on manager. He was in the field most days, looking at damaged cabinets containing electronics. He was at one location where, obviously, the cabinet had been underwater from the storm surge. All the electronics were completely ruined. Our plan was to build platforms that would allow us to elevate the equipment and protect it from future events. The property owner at that location came out and talked with our director. He said, "If you are going to raise that equipment, you better get it up pretty high."

The director asked, "How high did the water get here?"

The property owner immediately responded, "It was 23.4 feet!"

When the director relayed this story, he indicated that he was a bit shocked with the response. He said, "This man did not look like someone who would normally be dealing in decimals." So he asked, "And how do you know it was 23.4 feet?"

The man said, "Because I was in my boat, which was tied to my house. I used my depth finder!" He knew exactly how deep the water was.

We had a great laugh with that story.

There were many more stories, so many that I asked one of our staff employees to record them. We would refer back to them when we just needed a good laugh. It was not difficult to see how much a little laughter eased the stress on our employees, myself included.

Genuinely Care

It is difficult to motivate employees if there is a sense that the leadership does not genuinely care about them. People are our greatest asset! Leaders must demonstrate respect for the people in their organizations. We need to care about our employees!

Theodore Roosevelt said, "Nobody cares how much you know until they know how much you care."[1] Leaders should never forget this truth. It is essential that the leader genuinely cares about his/her employees. There are many examples of how this can be done, but I will share just a few that come to mind from some of my experiences.

In the utility industry, technicians work dangerous jobs. We placed a lot of emphasis on the importance of people working safely. The company safety slogan underscored this importance: "No job is so important and no task is so urgent that we cannot take time to perform our work safely." If we have a slogan, or a creed, we have to make sure that our conduct is consistent with it. We should genuinely care about our employees' safety and well-being.

We went to great lengths to measure our results. We had a scorecard where we measured over one hundred items. We seemed to find a way to measure everything numerically. The scorecard was used to measure our performance against other districts, and we were very competitive. We spent a lot of time analyzing those results and determining where improvements needed to be made. We had two items on the scorecard measuring employee safety, motor vehicle accidents, and personal injuries.

Once a month, we met with the union leadership. In one of those meetings, I was stressing the need to improve our results on safety. One of the union leaders told me, "The only reason you care about safety is because you care about the numbers."

I remember my response very clearly. I said, "I have learned that in this job, I will be criticized for my decisions. My push for improvements will not always be popular with all employees and certainly not with the union. I have learned to let some of that criticism roll off me.

However, this one I cannot just let roll off because it is not true.

"A little over a year ago, we all remember that one of our employees was killed in a tragic motor vehicle accident. Our driver was not at fault. I spent the next four days being present with his family members, ensuring they understood their benefits, providing them with my contact information, assuring them that I would be there for them, and just offering my sympathy and support. I did not think about the numbers even once during that time.

"Six months ago, I got a call from one of our managers late one evening. He told me that one of our technicians had a seizure and ran off the road in his company truck. He had been transported to the hospital and was in the emergency room. I left my house at 8:00 PM that night. I sat in the emergency room with the manager and the employee's wife and waited on a word from the medical staff on the employee's condition. I did not think one time about the numbers.

"So I am not taking that criticism because it is not true. It's not about the numbers. It's about people!"

I think that you could have heard a pin drop in the room. They knew that what I said was true. I think there might have even been a little embarrassment about the accusation.

Over the next few weeks, we met with all of the management team and presented our new safety slogan: It's About People! We had signs made for all our work centers, depicting the slogan. It helped us maintain the focus, and we were able to communicate that we cared about safety because we cared about our people. People can rally around that type initiative. Connecting the safety results to caring about people and their families motivates employees to work safely.

Value and Respect Every Employee

Respect for the individual employee is so important. Many people who are responsible for leading organizations have never recognized that fact. They are too wrapped up in their own self-interests and what can make them look good to their boss.

Late in my career, I had a boss who was late for every meeting. I never saw him be on time for a meeting or conference call. It was apparent that his strategy was for everyone to be waiting on him to start the meeting, and he would be able to make an entrance and have the entire focus be on him. It was one of the most prideful situations that I had ever seen and was totally disrespectful to every employee in the room or on the phone. Not surprisingly, when the meeting started, he was condescending to almost everyone who dared to have input. Most of the meetings involved other management people who were accustomed to it and did not get too ruffled by it. But it was still disrespectful, and the morale of the organization was the worst that I had seen in my career. It is critical for the leader to be on time, thereby respecting the other individuals in the meeting.

It is important for a leader to recognize that every employee can add value. When employees believe that they are valued and that their opinion counts, they are motivated and can help motivate their fellow employees. I have seen this happen in many instances over my career. Let me share a few illustrations.

In some of my early days of leading a team, we had monthly meetings to discuss ways to improve our trouble-causing telephone facilities. These meetings included all the supervisors who were reporting to me and would last as long as three or four hours. The technicians would complain about us being in meetings too often because the supervisors were sometimes tied up when they were needed in the field. As far as they were concerned, the meetings were a waste of time.

I decided that we would invite one technician to each month's meeting. We would rotate it around so that over six months, all groups would be represented. The guest technician was able to listen to us discuss and prioritize the actions that would be taken to correct problem-causing telephone-plant conditions over the next month. We saw that commitments were made and that accountability was expected of all the management employees in the room. As a reward for the technician sitting through the grueling meeting, he/she was asked to name the location in the field that was causing him/her the most trouble and adversely affecting his/her ability to perform the job efficiently. My commitment was that the situation would be repaired by the next month's meeting. This program was called Name It and Claim It.

Needless to say, the technicians loved the program. They liked being invited and trusted to provide input to the process. They were the best possible messengers back to their work group about how valuable the meetings were and how much good work was being done there.

As mentioned earlier, the damage from Hurricane Katrina was immense. In the copper telephone network, there are boxes where connections are made. Hundreds of these boxes went underwater. After the water receded, with low-voltage electricity over the copper wires, corrosion began to take place at the connection points in the boxes. The restoration procedures in place at that time called for you to pressure-wash the boxes with water and then spray an oily substance on the connection points. While it was not a long-term solution, the idea was that you could maintain service until you could replace the box with the permanent solution. I had charged one of our groups with implementing that cleaning process.

Still early into that process, we were at the dining tent one night, eating the evening meal. A technician who I had never met sat down across from me. I'm not sure if he knew my role or not, but most likely he did. He said, "I wonder who the idiot was that decided to have us spray the boxes with water. Everyone knows that water and electricity do not mix."

I said, "I guess that was me."

He said, "That is the dumbest thing I have ever heard."

I said, "It might be. What would you suggest that we do?"

He explained that he had mounted a sandblaster unit on his truck in the past and believed that we could blast the corrosion off the connectors with sand and not use water.

I said, "How many boxes can you do in a day?"

After agreeing on the size of an average box, he told me that he thought he could do two to three boxes a day.

I said, "Well, what are you waiting on?"

He was shocked that someone had actually listened to his idea and was willing to allow him to do it. I asked for pictures of his results and a daily update. It was a huge success!

After the restoration effort was complete, we wrote up his procedure and submitted it to headquarters for consideration and recognition. Needless to say, he was elated and felt pretty special. Regardless of their level, people want to be heard, and they have great ideas. If you never try their ideas, the generation of those ideas from that employee segment dries up, and they are not motivated to help in any way.

We had a lot of employees loaned from all over the Southeast to help with the Katrina restoration on the Mississippi Gulf Coast. Several employees were loaned from my home district of North Alabama. One of those employees was an outstanding technician who could outwork men half his age.

One Friday, after we were several months into the restoration, my phone rang; and it was the lineman. He said, "Someone told me that you like to eat catfish."

I assured him that I loved to eat fried catfish. He told me about a place that he and his coworker had found out in the country, about forty miles from the hotel he was staying at in Gulfport.

He said, "I told my buddy that if we drove that big line truck all the way up there just to eat dinner on Saturday night, you would probably fire us." I knew he was headed somewhere with the statement and just wanted to see where it would go.

I said, "You are probably right. I would have to consider that."

He said, "So I was just thinking. If we knew someone that liked catfish as much as us that could pick us up at the hotel after work on Saturday and drive us up there, we would not get in any trouble at all."

I thought it was great. I said, "What time will you be ready?"

He told me what time they would be finished with work and available to go on Saturday.

I said, "I will be there."

One of the guys on my staff and I left work on Saturday and picked them up at their hotel, and we enjoyed some really good catfish together. We had a great time! I'm not sure he knew how gratifying it was to me that he was comfortable enough with me to call and suggest such an outing.

People want to be respected! They respond to and trust leaders who act with humility. Ultimately, the benefits are apparent to both parties.

Certainly, we need to recognize good performance. We need to celebrate our accomplishments. We need to be cheerleaders as well as coaches. We need to regularly utilize two powerful words: *thank you*! A good practice is to start your day by finding someone to thank and end your day in the same manner. It will change your perspective, and it will certainly draw the attention of those who are on the receiving end of the appreciation. We have to be intentional if we are going to motivate employees in the organization.

CHAPTER 3

Performance

For many of us, our view of the workplace is shaped by our upbringing. I grew up on a small farm in North Mississippi. Actually, it was west of Guntown, in a little community called Cedar Hill. As I heard motivational speaker Charles Petty describe his hometown, Cedar Hill is on Highway 348, about halfway between Litter Barrel and Resume Speed. My dad taught me how to work at a young age. He taught me all about accountability. While it did not always seem beneficial at the time, I learned the importance of having a work ethic. I learned the importance of being dependable, someone that others could count on. He had high expectations, and it was clear to me that the chores would be done before I would be allowed to participate in athletic events or recreational activities. Those experiences seemed hard at the time, but it conditioned me for the rest of my life. And I would not have wanted it any other way. I value the experiences that I had growing up on the farm.

Commit to Win

The bottom line is this: I want to *win*! It is my nature! I do not apologize for the desire to win!

My desire to win was clearly passed along to my son, Will. When he was about six years old, Will was at a Wednesday-night class at our church. I stopped by at the end of the class to get him and take him home. When I looked in the door, I saw that he was crying. The teacher came out and talked with me. He said, "We were playing a game, and he lost." I told him that I was not surprised, and I apologized for Will's behavior.

On the way home, he was sitting in the back seat as I drove. I was talking with him pretty sternly, trying to help him understand that he had to control his emotions better. I told him that it was embarrassing for him to conduct himself that way just because he lost a game.

He said, "But, Dad."

I said, "Yes?"

He said, "When I win, it makes me feel good!"

We have laughed about that story over the years, and my family members have even used that phrase after our favorite team wins a ball game. It is true that when we win, it makes us feel good. It makes an organization feel good as well. An organization takes pride in winning, and it is up to the leader to set the tone and instill a winning culture.

Set Expectations and Instill Accountability

The key to achieving success in an organization is setting expectations and holding people accountable. As a leader, I always made sure my team understood that I was going to first hold myself accountable. I let them know that I would expect a sense of urgency from them but that they could expect the same from me. Displaying a sense of urgency is key in developing a winning culture. Employees have to understand that a lackadaisical approach to getting the job done is not acceptable. Procrastination is a poison that will destroy a team's ability to deliver a winning tradition.

This ability to hold people accountable does not always come naturally for the leader but can be developed over time. To develop the skill effectively, the leader must cast a clear vision and communicate clearly what success will look like for the team and for the individuals making up the team. Everyone should understand that both the team and the individuals must be serious about making their commitments.

I assumed responsibility for an organization that had been managed pretty loosely. I was very clear in the first meeting what would be expected, and it was very different from what had become routine for them. We were going through a reorganization at the time, and there was a voluntary offer to retire on the table for the management team. Following the meeting, I had a few people decide to take the offer. They just did not feel like they were going to be able to lead at the level I had described. It was the best decision for them, and I respected it. It was also the best decision for the organization. Their decisions made me confident that the expectations were understood.

Over the next several months, the accountability phase was experienced. Members of the management team were the ones struggling to deliver on the expectations. It was impossible to deal with poor performers in the technician ranks until the management team was all on board. There were a number of first-level managers who were just in the wrong job. We helped them move to positions in which they could succeed. But there were a few who just could not bring themselves to step up their game to an acceptable level. They simply could not hold their subordinates accountable to deliver the expected results. With as much grace as possible, the message to these managers was as follows: "I am not against you. I am for you. I want you to be in a job where you can succeed. But we have been very clear about how success looks, and you have not demonstrated an ability to get there. You will be placed on a development plan for the next sixty days, and we will help you, in every way, move your performance to an acceptable level. If you are not able to do that, you will be separated from the business."

While that message may sound harsh, it was honest, and it showed a level of accountability that most agreed was fair. Some moved their performance to an acceptable level. A few had to leave the business and I am confident were able to get into a line of work that was much more satisfying to them because they could perform it successfully.

When we met with one of the individuals who ended up exiting the business, he said, "Before you got here, the previous management would meet with us each month to review our results. They yelled and screamed at us. We left the meeting and went about business as usual. We came back in a month, nothing had changed, and we took another chewing. It just rolled off us. You did not yell and scream at us, but you meant everything you said and have followed through on it. It has just been different."

I share that story to give an illustration of how to instill accountability. It is fair to expect a high level of performance. As one of my first supervisors taught me, "people will perform at whatever level you will accept. If you accept substandard performance, that is all you will ever get." Throughout my career, I also found that people enjoy being part of a culture that has high expectations and celebrates winning. The leader sets the tone for what is acceptable and what is not. The leader has to be tough but tender and understanding.

We do not have to personally attack someone if they are just in the wrong job. In most cases, the employee in the wrong job is just as frustrated as the manager. The freedom that comes from being released from that vise is many times the best thing that could happen for them. But if the organization is going to reach its peak performance level, the leader cannot turn his/her head to mediocrity and let it continue.

I have vivid memories of another situation where I was trying to raise the expectations across the organization. We measured our performance on how long it took to repair the high-speed services for key customers.

In our staff meeting, I was insisting with my team and with one manager in particular that the time to repair the circuits had to improve.

He said, "I can make improvement, but it will take overtime. You aren't happy with our performance, but you aren't happy when I exceed my overtime budget. I had my car in the shop the other day, and the mechanic had a sign. The sign said, 'You can have it fast. You can have it cheap. You can have it done right. Pick two of the three.' That is what you need to understand. You can't have it all."

You could have heard a pin drop in the room as the other managers waited to see how I would respond to the gauntlet being thrown down.

I said, "I want all three. And if you want to work here, you will figure out a way to deliver all three."

The other managers thoroughly enjoyed the moment, and we all had a good laugh. The point is the leader has to set the expectations and hold the banner high. He/she cannot allow anyone to come up with excuses for why realistic goals cannot be achieved.

Going forward, that particular manager had some of the best repair times and best overtime results in the region. We celebrated those results, and he was proud of his team's accomplishments. It helps when the expectations are clear and there is no question about who will be accountable!

Utilize Humor Effectively

Speaking of the upbringing and productivity, I want to share a story from my days in Louisiana. We were placing a lot of emphasis on improving productivity. We measured our technicians by the number of tasks completed per day. I visited a work center early one morning and talked to the group. Obviously, one of the topics was productivity.

There was a technician in that group who had the highest productivity numbers in the state. Ironically, he went by the nickname Speedy. He did not want to be recognized in front of his coworkers. After the meeting, he was headed to his truck.

I pulled him aside and said, "Speedy, I looked at your numbers. You are knocking it out of the park. I just want you to know that I appreciate what you are doing."

He said, "I am just doing my job."

I said, "I know that, but I wanted you to know that I appreciate it."

He said, "I am going to tell you like my daddy always told me. If a man is going to pay you for eight hours a day, you ought to work as hard as you can…for at least six of them." When he paused near the end of that sentence, I thought I knew the rest of the quote. He laughed at the look on my face when he finished the sentence. I told him that if he could get that much work done in six hours, I was fine with that.

It is another example of humor in the right setting. When people feel good about their accomplishments, they are confident and are able to enjoy a good laugh. They are not intimidated by the leader being present.

Several years later, after I was working in Birmingham, we had a long-term project to position the company to be able to deliver high-speed Internet along with video over copper. The engineering component of the project was critical. We established a design center and awarded the detail work to an engineering contractor. We were just project-managing the output.

The manager of the operation came to me and showed how far behind the contractor had gotten. He had made repeated efforts to get them on track, but they just could not seem to get there. We called a meeting for their executive team. The owner of the company, who I had met several times before, decided to come with his team. There were probably about eight or ten of us in the conference room. The meeting was not contentious, but the firm knew that we were serious and were considering carving out some of the work and awarding it to some other firms.

Our engineering manager was well prepared and painted a clear picture of how far they were behind. We turned to the contract firm for a response. They communicated all the things they were doing to try to catch up, including their hiring and training of additional people. When they finished, I mentioned that all of that sounded good but that they were still behind, and I pressed them to tell me when they would be current. The next thing they said was probably not the best choice of words. The vice president said, "We are not where we want to be, but this work is hard."

I said, "Look, if it had been easy, we would have given it to one of your competitors!"

We all laughed, but the message had been delivered.

After the meeting, the owner followed me to my office and asked if he could have a word with me. He said that he had worked in the industry for over forty years and that was the best meeting he had ever attended. He appreciated that there was no yelling and screaming and that there was even some humor with the statement. He acknowledged that it was the first time that he had seen his vice president speechless. He told me that they would do whatever it took to get current with the work. And they did! The little bit of humor eased some of the tension, yet the point was made very clearly!

Fast-forward about ten years. I had retired from the company and was now working for a contract construction company. The company I worked for was asked if we could pick up some work in the Birmingham area that another company had failed to complete. We were eager to do that, and I went to a meeting to discuss it.

The person leading the meeting was the manager who had been responsible for the engineering in the previous story. He laid out a picture of the workload and said that all the projects needed to be completed by the end of the year. It was already August, and the amount of work was enormous.

I said, "That is a lot of work."

He leaned back in his chair and said, "Look, if this had been easy, I would have given it to one of your competitors!"

We had a good laugh. He told me that he had been hoping for the opportunity to tell me that. It was gratifying to me because I enjoyed seeing his skill at running a meeting and communicating his expectations but still displaying a sense of humor. He set the tone! By the way, we got the work done to his satisfaction!

Expect Operational Excellence

Strong teams understand the importance of executing the plan to perfection. Even the little things require our attention. The legendary coach Paul "Bear" Bryant said, "Little things make the difference. Everyone is well prepared in the big things, but only winners perfect the little things."[1]

I had a boss for a period of years who was an outstanding leader. He was very clear with his expectations and gave immediate feedback when coaching was needed. He had a saying that he used a lot, especially when we were preparing for emergency situations. He said, "Failing to plan is planning to fail." Leaders have to recognize the importance of being prepared with a microscopic attention to detail.

Employees in an organization always watch the leader to see if he/she is personally modeling what they are expecting the organization to do. In addition, they watch how the leader conducts business with other entities. Effective leaders are consistent with how they hold everyone to the same high standards.

Let me share a story that illustrates what I mean. During the restoration period on the Mississippi Gulf Coast following Katrina, my organization was dependent on a contract company to perform some pretty critical structural work where we were going to place electronic equipment. The project managers in our organization had become very frustrated with this particular company's inability to deliver anything that they had promised. The fact is that they had overcommitted and did not have nearly enough resources to manage the business they had taken on across all the areas in the Southeast affected by the storms. Repeated efforts had been made to get the company to respond to our needs. After multiple failures to deliver and continued broken promises, I asked their senior management to come to Gulfport and meet with my team.

It just turned out that the best day for my team to meet with them was on a Saturday, so that was when we scheduled the meeting and required their attendance. Now, you can imagine how thrilled they were to have to fly to Mississippi for a Saturday meeting. When we met, my team sat for a good while, listening to a lot of the same excuses that we had heard from their local management.

I had a copy of a small book by Elbert Hubbard entitled *A Message to Garcia*. I highly recommend this book if you have never read it. It paints a very clear picture of what it means to take ownership and accomplish a task while letting no obstacle get in your way and making no excuses in the time of it. I asked the highest executive in the room if he had ever read the book. He said he had not read it. I said, "Obviously not! I am going to do you a big favor.

I am going to give you this book. If you will read it, get your key managers to do the same and you practice what it says, I am confident you can lead your organization to deliver on its promises. You will not be able to salvage your business with us here because we are relieving you of all of that work today. But you might be able to earn someone else's trust!"

That may sound like a pretty harsh way to treat someone. But our people had tried every avenue possible to get the company to act on their commitments. They had failed repeatedly! I can assure you that the people in my organization left that room emboldened and appreciative of the support they had just received. They saw that not only was I going to have high expectations of them for the restoration effort but that I was also going to be consistent with those expectations for all that they were depending on to assist them in making it happen.

While it is a requirement of any business in a competitive environment, the drive for improvements in productivity always brings some amount of stress on the employees and also the leaders of an organization. Working with a unionized workforce produced an even heightened level of stress. I have already shared some of the discussions that we had around the challenges of working safely.

The union leadership contended that the emphasis on productivity was leading to poor safety results. It was their view that we were rushing our employees so much that they were taking shortcuts. Instead of just taking the opposing viewpoint, I wanted to determine if there was any truth to that argument. I asked my staff to study that hypothesis and determine if there was any substance to it.

The staff's research produced some interesting findings. They found that the organizations with the best productivity results also had the best safety results. That relationship held true at the district level, the manger level, the supervisor level, and the technician level. The results were overwhelmingly consistent. The data completely refuted the claim. Why is that?

The results on both productivity and safety were driven by pride on the part of the individual employees and how it affected their approach to the job. When that pride spread across employee groups and the entire organization, it helped foster a culture that demonstrated excellence in every aspect that one might measure.

Prioritize Appropriately

How can a focus on performance conflict with other components of the IMPACT model? There are two potential conflicts that will be discussed.

When a leader gets the team to a point where they are performing at a high level, the tendency is to hang on to all the people who are contributing to that success. Resist the urge to do that!

Early in my career, opportunities for advancement were almost nonexistent. I was working hard in an individual contributor role. I was enjoying my job. But I did have a desire to move into a leadership role and learn to manage a group. After about eight years, an opportunity came my way. I was promoted into a much more visible role that allowed me to expand skills and interface with many more people in the broader organization. I later learned that the only reason I was afforded that opportunity was because the operations manager in my organization was on vacation. Apparently, he had squelched previous inquiries about my availability and would have this one as well had he not been on vacation. In fact, when he returned from vacation and found out about my opportunity, he called me and tried to convince me that I should not be interested in the new position.

Why would he do that? He did it because he was pleased with my performance and knew that I was valuable to his results. He had a selfish viewpoint and was more interested in his own success than he was in mine.

I told myself at that moment that if I was ever in a position of leading an organization, I would not treat people in that manner. I believe that I held true to that commitment. I helped employees who had potential and wanted to expand their skill sets to move into other positions that would help them accomplish their goals. It is important for leaders to develop the employees in their organizations and help them in their career advancement. Leaders have to be intentional about this because the natural tendency is to protect themselves. It is a compliment to your organization if people want to hire or promote your people.

The philosophy described here can be referred to as winning at any cost. Some people have a level of success with that philosophy. My contention is that it will be a short-term success. If winning means treating people with disrespect, it is not possible to maintain a winning culture over the long-haul.

People in your organization need to know that if they perform at a high level, that performance will be recognized and rewarded. Part of that reward is that they will be developed and pushed toward advancement and further development opportunities, not shielded from them. That culture helps improve performance and helps keep the entire organization motivated at a high level. Conversely, if employees notice that no matter how hard they work and no matter how successful the organization becomes, they are stuck in their current position, they are not motivated and will burn out at some point. The desired performance will deteriorate over time. Selfish leaders do not see this, but it is a fact.

When the overwhelming focus of the leader is on performance and winning, there is another danger to the organization. Constant pressure to deliver results can cause employees to conclude that they must do whatever it takes to meet the desired objective. In many cases, it can drive the employee to compromise his/her integrity by cheating to get the results. Leaders have to be conscious of this fact. For starters, goals must be realistic. They should be achievable with a reasonable amount of hard work.

I was fortunate to have a mentor who helped me understand this potential conflict shortly after I had stepped into a key leadership position. We were constantly pressing our technicians to deliver the expected number of tasks per day. My friend called me "Little Brother." He was serious about delivering results, and he knew that I was too. In fact, we were extremely competitive. He told me one day, "Little Brother, we have to be very careful how much pressure we put on our people to deliver the targets because they will do whatever it takes to make the numbers, and that includes cheating." That comment stuck with me.

There has to be a balance in the components of the model that could be in conflict. From that point on, I told my team that I would push hard for results. But I also told them not to ever conclude that I wanted them to cheat to achieve those results. I made it clear in every discussion that I would never ask them to compromise their integrity. In fact, it there is a conflict between integrity and any other component of the IMPACT model, integrity must always win!

CHAPTER 4

Attitude

Attitude is so important. I believe that I am responsible for and in control of my attitude. I cannot allow someone else to shape my attitude. That is the premise with which I tried to start every day of my career. Yes, pressures and distractions are sure to come. Days hardly ever seem to go the way you had planned them. But we are able to control how we manage through those challenges, and we do not have to let our attitudes turn sour.

Attitudes are key to how well we work with others. Interpersonal relationships can certainly be challenging at times. I always said, "If I can't get along with someone, it's my fault." I have to take the responsibility for making relationships work.

Be Positive

I like a positive atmosphere. The late General Colin Powell said, "Perpetual optimism is a force multiplier."[1] If we are not careful, we can fall into the trap of complaining because we don't have enough resources to accomplish what we are expected to do. Instead of complaining about what we don't have, we need to focus on what we *can* do with what we *do* have. According to General Powell, if an organization has a positive attitude, it seems like you have more resources than you actually do.

One way to keep your attitude positive is to recognize the value of having a job in the first place. If you have been entrusted with a leadership position, it is even more appropriate to have an appreciation for the opportunity. Being thankful for the job at the beginning of every day helps shape your attitude and prepares you for effectively leading others.

I don't have a lot of time for folks being negative. Don't allow yourself to swim in a sea of negativity. I have seen organizations that have fostered a negative culture. Fairly early in my career, one part of the state that I worked in was known for having a negative attitude. It was just depressing to go there, and I did not want to be there long. It was contagious. People with negative attitudes feed on one another. It is especially easy for new employees to get pulled into that type culture. It happens without the employee even realizing it.

My low tolerance for negativity and whining was developed early on, shaped to a large extent by my high school football coach, who did not tolerate whining. Willis Wright was one of the winningest football coaches in Mississippi history and was recently inducted into the Mississippi Sports Hall of Fame. I had the honor of playing for him early in his career. Whenever anyone complained about anything, like running wind sprints, he had one simple phrase: "Life in itself is tough." That simple phrase communicated how little interest he had in hearing a player whine. And he was right! Life is tough!

Those words stuck with me throughout my career. We run into all kinds of obstacles at work and in life that could cause us to want to quit. If we allow ourselves to do it, it is easy to slip into a mode of whining, complaining, and adopting a negative attitude. Allowing that to happen makes it so much more difficult to succeed.

I am not interested in listening to excuses about why something cannot be done. I would prefer that the leaders in an organization spend their time discussing how it can be done. The perception of an organization is formed by how well they get things done, how willing they are to help others, and how well they keep their commitments. Leaders should expect his/her employees to become a can-do organization. If he/she expects to lead a can-do organization, he/she must be a can-do leader. The employees will catch the can-do attitude from the leader.

Practice Humility

Humility has to be the overarching attitude of the leader. The Turknett Leadership Group says, "People who demonstrate humility don't think less of themselves; they just think more of others."[2] We have to admit our own faults and limitations.

Some leaders are so wrapped up in themselves that they cannot grasp the importance of displaying humility.

Truthfully, it is an attribute that does not come naturally. It takes an intentional effort to practice humility, but it is well worth the investment.

Many leaders are much more consumed with letting their employees know how much they know. They are convinced they are the smartest person in the organization because they are the boss. When that is what is driving him/her, the employees quickly realize it, and the leader loses credibility. David Abney, retired CEO of UPS, described it best when he said, "Throughout my career, I have been fortunate to have had interactions with many incredibly smart people, some of whom are well aware of how smart they are and want everyone else to acknowledge them as the smartest person in the room. My guidance to those individuals is if you are the smartest person in the room, you do not have to prove that to everyone else. They will recognize it. Really smart people are also excellent listeners that are just as interested in learning from others as they are in teaching them."[3]

Most of us have seen leaders who have a large ego and never mastered an attitude of humility. In one organization of which I was a part, an executive stood in front of some very capable middle-level managers and declared that there was a reason that some people were located at headquarters and making the decisions. In a nutshell, he said it was because they had the most knowledge and the best plan. He indicated that everyone else just needed to focus on executing that plan. He showed no interest in hearing ideas from the employees in the room. There was no humility evident in this particular leader on this occasion or any other occasion that I had the opportunity to observe him. Needless to say, the people in the room immediately lost whatever respect that his position should have commanded.

One component of displaying humility is having the ability to laugh at oneself. Many leaders are so uptight that they are never able to relax enough to display this very important attribute. Their people are equally uptight and always careful not to cross the line. That culture of everyone walking on eggshells harms the effectiveness of an organization. The leader can calm all that tension by being able to laugh at himself/herself.

One situation sticks out in my mind that highlights this point. Midway in my career, I had received a promotion and had taken on a significant level of responsibility in North Louisiana. We were in the second half of the fiscal year and were experiencing an expense crunch. Several expense-reduction measures had been put in place, including the decision to suspend maintenance tree trimming for a period of time.

I had been in this particular job for about two weeks when I received a call from my immediate supervisor. He proceeded to grill me for some tree-trimming expenditures that occurred in the previous month. He knew that I had not been at the helm when this occurred, but that was not the point. He said, "Did you not hear the message to stop tree-trimming? You need to make sure that your people understand the directive and that there is no more of it."

I assured him that I understood, would investigate where it occurred, and make the necessary corrections. He was pretty fired up, and it did not seem an appropriate time to point out that I was not in charge the previous month.

When the conversation with my supervisor had ended, I called my cohort and mentor in the neighboring district. I asked if he had received a call. He said he had not and asked what was up. I explained the situation to him. He thanked me and was off to check to see if his district had any occurrences of tree trimming so he could be prepared for a similar call. Nothing else was said, and the issue was over.

Our staff meeting was the next week, held by video conference instead of in person, again, to save on travel expense. The video conference began, and the boss conducted a roll call to make sure that everyone was on. When the camera switched to my friend, all you could see was greenery all around him. He had pulled every artificial plant in the building into the video room. When he answered the roll call, he was pulling back branches to reveal that he was actually in the room.

The boss asked, "What is that around you?"

My friend responded, "Well, unlike some districts, we have not been able to do any tree trimming in our district."

We all laughed, including the boss. While the joke was on me, I think I found it funnier than anyone else. To some degree, it showed me that I had been accepted into the group, and it set the stage for a most enjoyable working relationship.

Get Personally Involved

Employees need to see that the leader enjoys what he/ she does and doesn't mind doing some insignificant tasks. I will give you an example. Over the years, our company had gotten lax on the security at our work locations. Gates were being left unlocked during the day, and trucks were being left unlocked at the end of the day. People without identification might wander onto our property and not be challenged by the employees. Needless to say, it was pretty loosely managed.

The executives cracked down pretty hard and made it clear that the issue was serious. I had a conversation with my subordinates about the need to get some discipline around the issue. I challenged them to get out and look at their locations and make sure things were tightened up. I also told them that I would make some surprise visits to random locations in each district to perform inspections.

One of the directors said, "You know that once the word gets out that you are in the field, everyone will be tipped off, and you will not see the real picture."

I said, "You may be right." I did not tell him at the time, but I took that as a personal challenge!

I told my staff manager that he and I would make the visits at night. He was intrigued by the idea and laid out the plan. We started at dusk in South Florida and visited locations throughout the night. After getting a little sleep, we traveled north in the daytime and visited work locations in Orlando, Daytona, and Jacksonville the next evening. In all, we visited three work-center locations in each of the four districts in the state. We found glaring problems at almost every location, and very few people ever knew we were there. The employees we happened upon were sworn to secrecy.

When we covered my subordinates on the findings, I asked them if any knew we were in the state. They had to admit that they did not and were a little embarrassed. The points were made about the security gaps at the work centers, and they got busy with the corrections. We all had a good laugh about the surprise approach taken. It helps to foster a good environment where everyone can have a good laugh.

But the seriousness of the situation was not lost upon anyone, and I think they respected the attitude of their leader. It gave them more clout when they were communicating to their employees the seriousness of the situation. Sometimes it is just advantageous to do things that are innovative, out of the norm. It provides a little spark to the organization and helps it move to where you are trying to go.

Embrace Change

One of the biggest obstacles in maintaining a positive attitude is dealing with change. Change is pretty constant no matter what industry you are in. Change may be driven by external factors such as competition, the economic climate, the political climate, or customer expectations. It may be driven by internal factors such as changes in procedures, policies, or employee benefits. Regardless of the driver, change is a part of the business and, furthermore, our lives.

We will never be able to reach our potential unless we are willing to change. Even better, we much embrace change. Someone has said, "Success will come to those who learn to love chaos and change, not to those who try to avoid it."[4] I have found that truth to be applicable to so many situations in my business career. You may be thinking, *Why should I learn to love chaos?* or *I will never love change.* It is important to recognize that change is like a freight train that is coming down the track. There is nothing we can do to stop it. If we try to stand against it, it is going to lead to frustration and will ultimately run over you.

If a leader is always bucking against change, he/she will become completely ineffective. It makes more sense to accept the reality and lead the team to make whatever adjustments are necessary to adapt and even flourish with the change.

When trying to drive change, a leader should recognize that several conditions must be met. If any of these components are lacking, real change will not be realized. The model shown here is the best depiction that I have seen on the subject. This model was produced by the late Dr. Darrell T. Piersol, Distinguished Professor of Management, Emeritus, at Southwest Texas State University.[5]

Managing Complex Change

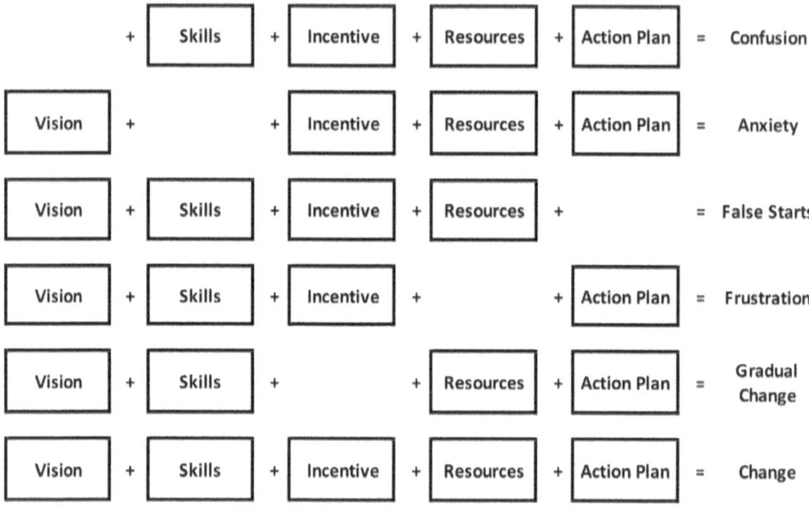

Dr. Derrell T. Piersol
Distinguished Professor of Management Emeritus
Southwest Texas State University

Leaders must evaluate these components and understand that there can be no shortcuts if real change is to be realized. Change cannot be forced upon an organization just because the leader declares it. If any of the components of this model are missing, real change will not materialize, and employee attitudes will suffer as a result. Employees struggle when they are asked to do something and do not have the ability to pull it off for whatever reason. On the other hand, if the leader has planned properly and the key components are in place, real change can be affected, and positive attitudes will flourish as employees understand that change may not be so bad.

When leaders are looking for people to hire, they should be looking at those who exhibit proper attitudes. The late Herb Kelleher, former CEO of Southwest Airlines, understood this fact and said it this way: "We look for attitudes: people with a sense of humor who don't take themselves too seriously. We'll train people on whatever it is they need to do, but the one thing Southwest cannot change in people is inherent attitudes."[6]

It is the leader's job to create an environment where people can learn and grow, but each employee is responsible for his/her own attitude. We decide what it will be!

CHAPTER 5

Communication

Communication is one of the most difficult things for leaders to practice effectively. Most leaders rose to higher positions in companies by becoming proficient and proving themselves in the intricate details of the industry. Whether it be in finance, technology, or maybe manufacturing, they have excelled well enough to earn a position of responsibility. In many cases, those individuals have never learned how to communicate.

In the telecommunications industry, many leaders who had risen through the ranks were people who enjoyed field jobs and had never been taught the importance of effective communication. The art of communication does not come naturally. Leaders have to work at it daily and need to be reminded of its importance.

Communicate Clearly

Leaders are charged with communicating the mission to the organization. They must explain why it is important.

We can't expect our folks to know things if we do not tell them. Let's not assume that they know. It is easy for leaders to sit in the office and in conference rooms and map out the plan. We come back, revisit it, and tweak it to where we feel good about it. We talk about it so much in our small circles that we are convinced that everyone understands it just as well as we do. It is a critical error that is made multiple times over.

No strategy is complete until the communication plan is developed and then executed. General George S. Patton said, "The soldier must know what he is doing at all times. He must know the objective."[1]

Speaking of being clear, I am reminded about a time when my daughter, Allyson, was in kindergarten. It was the season of Thanksgiving, and her teacher at the church kindergarten had divided the class into two groups to reenact the first Thanksgiving: Pilgrims and Native Americans. To help the children with their roles, they were all given names. Allyson was a Native American, and she came home and told us that the teacher had assigned them names.

We said, "What is your name?"

She said, "My name is Little Telephone."

We found that interesting and began to quiz her about it. We found that the teacher had told her that her name would be Little Fawn. Allyson, who clearly knew the industry her dad worked in, thought she said Little Phone.

While that was a humorous story to us, it underscores how easily words can be misunderstood. Employees are sometimes like Allyson. They are too embarrassed to ask for clarification, or they think they should know and understand what was said. The leader assumes that everyone understands clearly and is off to other items without actually checking to ensure the message was received.

Communicate Truthfully

Another pitfall in communication from leaders is that they tend to attempt to find a way to tell people what they want to hear. They look for ways to soften bad news. While there can be some merit to that, most of the time, leaders should communicate the facts. In some instances, by the time the message is filtered and softened by the leader, it loses its real meaning; and the recipient is left wondering about what was being said.

Leaders should make sure that the true message is being communicated. Sometimes hard messages have to be delivered. It is imperative that we are honest with employees. Even if it is bad news, employees can handle most things if they know they are receiving honest communication and that their leadership is being transparent with them.

Don't just talk for the sake of talking. You have all met individuals that statement describes. They can talk forever, and at the end, you are left wondering, "What did he/she just say?" I am reminded of the way that I heard an individual described one time. It was said that his mother talked all the time and that his daddy never said anything. He took after both of them! We don't need to be that way. We need to have some content in what we talk about. When we finish, no one should be wondering what we said.

Close the Feedback Loop

Communication does not always mean talking. It also means listening. I always liked to ask technicians to tell me about challenges they were experiencing on the job, things that were keeping them from being able to perform the job efficiently. When you open up the door to hear from employees, you have to be ready to take action on what they give you. If you do not act on some of the items you are given, you quickly lose credibility. And an important part of communication is getting back with them on what was done.

Let me give an example of what I mean. Soon after I began to work in a new position in Birmingham, I visited with a group of maintenance technicians in a work center. It was my first visit in this particular location and their first opportunity to meet me. After talking for fifteen or twenty minutes about our focus and expectations, I opened it up for questions and comments. I encouraged them to share whatever they would like. One technician in the back of the room began to tell me about a defective section of cable that had become almost impossible to maintain. He told me that a new section of cable had been placed a few years earlier but that the service had never been cut over to the new cable by construction. I asked for some details on the location, wrote them down, and told him that I would look into it. His next comment struck hard. He said, "Whatever you do, don't tell me that you will get back to me because I know that is not true. I've been told that before."

While I knew that he was not talking about me personally, I also knew that he could have been. How many times had I taken a problem from an employee, maybe even solved that problem, but had never taken the time to give feedback on the resolution? We have to complete the feedback loop.

You can rest assured that I began checking on that situation as soon as I returned to the office. I need to digress a bit here because there is also a lesson in this illustration on integrity. A few years earlier, the new cable had been placed. The workload was heavy at the time for construction, so they were unable to complete that particular job, splice the new cable, and perform the cutover. One of the measurements for construction performance was overage jobs, or cycle time. Because the job was old and hurting their results, the construction manager made the decision to close the job. He reported the work as complete, but it was never done. That is the reason the new cable had been placed but never spliced.

Once again, we should be cautious about what we measure and how much pressure we put on people to deliver. Too much emphasis and pressure can cause people to compromise their integrity by lying to look better on the measures and get the heat off.

I instructed engineering to reissue the job and for the construction group to promptly splice the cable, cut the working service to it, and remove the old trouble-causing cable. All of that was done in less than a week.

I made another visit to the work center and stood in front of the entire group. I told the technician who had surfaced the issue, "I know you indicated that you did not believe that I would get back with you. But the old cable you told me about is no longer there. Service is now working through the new cable."

He said, "I know. I saw the construction group finishing it a day or two ago."

Leaders should not underestimate the importance of feedback. There was value in taking that employee's complaint seriously, looking into it, resolving it, and then providing the feedback. That is an example of how leaders can establish credibility. Every employee needs to feel important. We can help them know they are important if we listen to them and then show them the respect of following up and giving them feedback. Leaders should look for opportunities to demonstrate the ability to communicate in this manner.

That experience made such an impact on me that I began to look for ways to incorporate the concept into daily practice. An individual on my staff had strong expertise in database software. He was able to develop a mechanized tool where technicians could input an issue that was causing them difficulty. They were required to provide a sufficient amount of detail and select the group they thought could own the issue. When they entered the information and saved it, the system would automatically send an email to a previously identified recipient in the appropriate organization. That individual was responsible for running the issue to ground and determining the solution. He/she would input the solution and a time frame to the database. The initiator could look at any time to check the status.

The management team could print reports of open issues and closed issues. A feedback mechanism was available to all, and I had the opportunity to monitor the activity.

We named the tool the ALERT database, which stood for Always Looking to Eliminate Roadblocks Together. This is just one example where a number of people got involved and placed a priority on giving feedback, driven by one simple situation where a single technician had been disappointed by poor communication from previous leaders. I will always contend that sometimes fixing the little things that may seem insignificant can have a huge impact on an organization.

Again, effective leaders make clear communication, including listening, a priority. It may sound like a simple, mundane task. But communication is something that cannot be delegated. Clear communication must come from the leader, and it has to happen on a regular basis.

CHAPTER 6

Teamwork

Teamwork drives success! Unfortunately, in today's world, teamwork is another quality that does not seem to come naturally. People feel a need to differentiate themselves from their peers. Leadership training even encourages those who desire to advance to determine ways to make themselves stand out from the rest of the pack. While all of that is well intended, individuals sometime conclude that he/she has to do that at the expense of the team. That is a terrible misconception. It is the leader's responsibility to ensure that the organization places a high value on teamwork.

Leaders who excel at getting a team to work together for a common goal will enjoy significant success and heightened morale in the organization. When teamwork is a priority, the team members will learn how to support one another, help one another, encourage one another, learn from one another, and, if need be, defend each other. They will elect to do the right thing for the team. Most of the time, that will be the same as for their individual good. Sometimes it may not be.

Value Every Team Member

I have always believed in participative management. I value the opportunity to have a group of experts in a room to discuss a problem and arrive at the best solution. Ken Blanchard says, "None of us are as smart as all of us."[1] This has been a favorite quote of mine since I read *High Five!*—one of Blanchard's many books on leadership. It captures the essence of why I think each person's viewpoint should be heard. It is important that each team member involved in this type of meeting understands that his/her thoughts are desired. Everyone should feel a freedom to express their ideas, even those who might have a minority viewpoint.

In one organization of which I was a part, we had a list of operating principles. One of the principles was "an obligation to dissent." That is not a license to be negative about every subject. But it does mean that if you have a differing opinion from the dominant one in the room, you should feel compelled and free to express your concern. If every thought is lifted up, the team is much more likely to come to the right decision. There is no way that one person can know as much or consider as many alternatives as a group of experienced people.

There is another important aspect of these type meetings, though. Once everyone's voice has been heard and the team has made a decision, that decision must be supported by everyone when they leave the room. It is essential that the employees in an organization observe a leadership team that is in lockstep. People will naturally look for a crack, trying to find an open critic to the decision that was made in the room. There can be no tolerance of leaks or dissent once a decision is made.

The effective leader recognizes that each individual team member is important and valuable to the team. Phil Jackson, maybe the greatest NBA coach of all time, said, "The strength of the team is each individual member. The strength of each member is the team."[2]

I have shared a story over the years to illustrate this point. On spring break one year, my family went to Colorado on a snow-skiing trip. It was our first time, so we had a lot to learn. We all signed up for ski lessons. Let me just say that our teenage girls did extremely well. My wife and I did not excel at skiing. Since Will, my son, was only five years old at the time, he stayed at a day care center. They took them out once or twice during the day and gave some beginner classes for skiing.

Back at the condo, on the first evening, while we were having dinner, each family member shared about his/her day. When it came to Will's turn, he shared that he did not like the cold. He did not enjoy being outside during the lessons because it made his head hurt. I knew there were hundreds of children out there. I asked him how his teachers kept up with them.

He said, "They divided us into teams. But we lost one little boy in our team. His name was Pierre."

We were pretty shocked by that fact.

Someone changed the subject, and we moved on to another conversation without hearing any more about it.

The next morning, I was walking Will back down to the daycare center. I said, "Will, how many people are on your team?"

He kept walking straight ahead and said, "Seven, if they found Pierre."

It was a funny story and one that I enjoyed telling the rest of the family. It never occurred to me the night before that, that he was not sure whether they had found Pierre. I am sure they did. But I thought about how easy it is for us to just forget about a teammate who might be the quiet one in the group. His/her job might seem insignificant to some, and it is easy to take him/her for granted. We do not need to let that happen! Every team member is important! We do not need to lose Pierre!

Take the Initiative to Help

We have examined some theoretical aspects of team-work. You may be wondering how this component of the model plays out in the real world. Let me give you an example. In fact, I will illustrate the difference between good teamwork and bad teamwork.

In the telecommunications industry—or in any utility industry, for that matter—you are constantly challenged by weather events. The common events are tornadoes, hurricanes, and ice storms. Right after Christmas 2000, I was still relatively new in a position, having assumed responsibility for a large geography in North Louisiana. A large ice storm struck across the northern part of the state. We were scrambling to find enough generators to keep service up across the network. In addition, we knew that we did not have enough people to maintain acceptable service levels.

My peer in central Louisiana was not hit by the storm. Nevertheless, he was plugged in to what was occurring. He initiated the phone call to me. It went something like this: "Hey, Little Brother. My people are loading up generators in our yards right now. They will be headed your way in just an hour or two. I am also getting volunteers for technicians who are willing to go there and work. I will send you all that I can afford to send."

I cannot appropriately convey how good it felt to get that phone call. He and I were extremely competitive in all our results. He wanted to beat me on every measure if he could, and I felt the same about him. But when the chips were down, teamwork prevailed. Teamwork took priority! What a good feeling it gave our boss to know that we would work that way as team! He knew we were competitive, but he also knew we could be counted on to help each other when needed.

I hung on to those people as long as I could. In fact, after a few weeks, when we almost had service back to normal levels, I was still using the thirty or so people that he had loaned me. He called me one morning and said, "Hey, Pharaoh. This is Moses! I need you to let my people go!" We had a good laugh and made arrangements for them to return home. I learned a lot from my teammate in that experience. That is how teamwork should work!

Just a few years later, I was in a similar job in another location. Some storms had come through, and we just could not dig out from under the heavy workload. While my peer knew the situation, I did not receive a call with an offer to help. After a few days, I initiated a call to him. I asked, "Is there any way that you could spare a few people for a week or so to help me out?" The plea was rejected even though he was able to handle his workload while working little to no overtime.

I share that to illustrate the difference in the two approaches. An organization either has a commitment to teamwork, or it has a commitment to selfishness. It is not hard to determine which one enjoys success and high morale and which one wallows in mediocrity.

A strong leader insists on having on the team the type of individuals who understand the importance of teamwork. He/she should demand the type approach modeled in the first example above. It should be clearly understood before the crisis comes. It is just as crucial for the leader to be prepared to address any individual on the team who demonstrates the attitude described in the second example. In times of crisis, the team should pull together and abandon self-interests. I am grateful to say that over my career, I saw many more instances like the first example.

Why is teamwork so important? The obvious answer is that the overall good of the larger organization takes precedent. But an added benefit is that when employees in each organization observe little things like those described above, it shapes his/her approach to daily activities. People have a desire to be on a winning team! And they are proud when their leaders provide leadership by displaying teamwork!

CHAPTER 7

Making an Impact

In 2000, Mississippi State and Texas A&M played in the Independence Bowl. Because of an unusual weather event in Shreveport, the game became known as the Snow Bowl. I graduated from Mississippi State, and it was a unique experience for me to have my team play in a bowl game in the town where I was living. One of the engineering managers who I worked with was a Texas A&M graduate. He invited me to attend a breakfast for the two teams and fans sponsored by the Fellowship of Christian Athletes. We enjoyed attending the event together.

Both teams were well represented, with players and coaches in attendance. Both head coaches spoke, and so did star players from each team. But the comments from one speaker stood out from the rest. The speaker was Dr. Rick Rigsby, who at the time was chaplain of the Texas A&M football team. He talked about how they challenged their student athletes to make an *impact* on the football field. However, the emphasis was not just on their performance on the field. The athletes were encouraged to make an *impact* in the classroom, in the workforce after graduation, and in the communities in which they would live. He explained that their student athletes were challenged to make an *impact* wherever they were for the rest of their lives.

He went on to say that there is a difference between making an impression and making an impact. An impression is temporary in nature. It will have a short-term effect. An impact is a permanent influence. It will have a long-term effect. It may be life-changing. [1]

You and I can probably agree that many leaders today want to make an impression on people. Their entire focus is to impress those with whom they come into contact. The desire seems to be to make a quick impression and move on to the next challenge. On the other hand, the *real* leaders desire to make an impact on those they are responsible for leading. It takes time and an investment to make an impact on someone.

The Snow Bowl happened to occur during the time that I was working to hammer out my leadership philosophy. As I began to try to put my leadership philosophy into words, I kept coming back to that word *impact*. I remembered Dr. Rigsby's challenge of the need to impact people's lives. I knew that is what I wanted to do as a leader. I then began to realize that the leadership components I had written down could actually form an acrostic of the word *impact*. At that time, I knew the following values were essential for my philosophy: integrity, attitude, communication, and teamwork. Once I realized that I wanted to hinge it around the word *impact*, the word *performance* came pretty naturally. I will admit that I had to think about it for a while to settle on *motivation*. But I do not think it is a stretch.

I knew that I had landed on a model that depicted the leadership traits that I deemed important. I also knew that it fit my desired criteria of being something simple enough that I could remember it and talk about it. Over the next several years, I shared the model with each organization that I had the privilege to lead. I found that people received it quite well and embraced the concept. The need to make an impact on people resonated with them.

As I shared it with my teams, the model popped up on bulletin boards around the country. Some short phrases like "Let's not forget about Pierre" were written as reminders on bulletin boards by members of local teams. I realized that people could rally around these really simple truths.

Do I have this mastered? Absolutely not! It takes work every day. I firmly believe that the way I respond to situations today is based, to a large degree, on the experiences that I've had in the past. So every day I learn new things. I build on that experience. And if I practice the things that we've talked about, I get better. After all, that should be the goal!

There is a Greek word—*oikos*—that means "house," "home," or "family,"—the people around us, our sphere of influence.[2] We all have an *oikos*. There are a number of people in your sphere of influence. You have the opportunity to provide them leadership. You have the opportunity to make an *impact* on their lives. We should strive to be the best that we can be so that we can make the right kind of *impact* on the people in our sphere of influence, our *oikos*.

We learn from good leaders! We learn equally as much from bad leaders! I was very fortunate in that I worked for some great leaders. Yes, I worked for one or two that were not good leaders at all. But I learned something from them all!

As I said at the beginning, there is nothing new in the model. It is simple! It had to be so that I could remember, communicate, and practice it. All I can tell you is that it works! Any problem, any day, you can apply the model.

Becoming a strong leader takes work. It takes practice and a commitment to get better every day. I encourage you to incorporate the components of this model into your daily practices and discover for yourself *Leadership That Makes an Impact*!

Chapter 1
1   Robert and Carolyn Turknett, Turknett Leadership Group, *The Leadership Character Model* (Atlanta, Georgia: 2005).
2   John Morley, British writer and newspaper editor, https://allgreatquotes.com.
3   David Axelrod, *Patton on Leadership* (Paramus, New Jersey: Prentice Hall Press, 1991), 100.

Chapter 2
1   Theodore Roosevelt, late United States president, www.braineyquote.com.

Chapter 3
1   Creed and Heidi Tyline King, *I Ain't Never Been Nothing but a Winner: Coach Paul "Bear" Bryant's 323 Greatest Quotes about Success, on and off the Football Field* (Lanham, Maryland: Taylor Trade Publishing, 2001), 113.

Chapter 4
1   Amy Nakamura, "'Leadership is Solving Problems': General Colin Powell's Rules for Leadership and More," *USA Today*, October 18, 2021.
2   Robert Turknett and Carolyn Turknett, Turknett Leadership Group, *The Leadership Character Model* (Atlanta, Georgia, 2005)
3   David Abney, verbal conversation with author, November 2022.
4   Anonymous.
5   Dr. Darrell T. Piersol, Distinguished Professor of Management Emeritus at Southwest Texas State University in San Marcos, Texas.
6   Jackie Freiberg and Kevin Freiberg, *Nuts!: Southwest Airlines Crazy Recipe for Business and Personal Success* (Austin, Texas: Bard Press, 1996), 67.

Chapter 5
1   David Axelrod, *Patton on Leadership* (Paramus, New Jersey: Prentice Hall Press, 1991), 92.

Chapter 6
1   Ken Blanchard, Sheldon Bowles, Don Carew and Eunice Parisi-Carew, *High Five* (New York, New York: HarperCollins Publishers, 2001), 184.
2   Phil Jackson, retired NBA Coach, www.wisesayings.com.

Chapter 7

1 Dr. Rick Rigsby, Independence Bowl Fellowship of Christian Athletes Breakfast 2001, Shreveport, Louisiana.

2 Thomas Addington and Stephen Graves, "Vocational Oikos," https://:worklife.org.

ABOUT THE AUTHOR

Carl Basden spent his career in telecommunications with South Central Bell, BellSouth, and AT&T. He spent most of his career in the network organization, ascending to various positions of leadership and ultimately becoming an assistant vice president of AT&T. He led large organizations with responsibilities in engineering, construction, installation, and maintenance. His final job with AT&T was in fleet management, where he led the organization responsible for the repair and maintenance of AT&T's fleet. After retiring from AT&T, he worked for four years as a division vice president with MasTec Inc., with responsibilities in telecommunications.

Carl is a native of Mississippi. He holds a bachelor's degree in civil engineering from Mississippi State

University and has an MBA from Mississippi College. After living and working in a number of places throughout the South, Carl and his wife, Sharia, currently reside in Starkville, Mississippi. They have three children and a growing number of grandchildren. He enjoys traveling, golf, and woodworking in his spare time.

www.ingramcontent.com/pod-product-compliance
Lightning Source LLC
Chambersburg PA
CBHW031500150726
47990CB00007B/2826